Wide Awake

Copyright © 2016 by Emily Marko

All rights reserved. No part of this book may be reproduced in any form or by any electronic or mechanical means, including information storage and retrieval systems, without permission in writing from the author.

All rights reserved. No part of this publication may be reproduced, distributed, or transmitted in any form or by any means, including photocopying, recording, or other electronic or mechanical methods, without the prior written permission of the publisher or author, except in the case of brief quotations embodied in critical reviews and certain other noncommercial uses permitted by copyright law. For permission requests, email the publisher or author at info@oneideapress.com.

To contact the publisher, visit www.OneIdeaPress.com
To contact the author, visit www.EmilyMarko.com

ISBN-13: 978-1-944134-11-2
ISBN-10: 1-944134-11-5

Printed in the United States of America

Headshot: Cindy Hines

Wide Awake

A 7-Day Visual Guide
TO CALM THE MIND + GET THE SLEEP YOU DESERVE

by Emily Marko

Why I Wrote This Book

I remember a far off time when sleeping wasn't something I even thought about; it just happened when I needed it to. But then, **LIFE** happened—kids, families, jobs, responsibilities, relationships, conflicts—and my brain didn't always know how to handle it all. So began decades of struggling to find sleep. Never would I have called myself an "insomniac."

Seems a bit intense for me, but by definition, that is exactly what I was: A person who suffers from insomnia has the inability to obtain sufficient sleep, through difficulty in falling or staying asleep.

I tried several methods over the years to find my sleep again. I practiced mindful breathing techniques, drank chamomile tea or a glass of wine in the evening, I ate dinner earlier in the day, tried reading before bed, tried not reading before bed, turned off electronics, wore a sleep mask, used aromatherapy oils, and the list goes on. Sometimes it worked. Often, it did not.

Then, in 2010, I began my work in visual thinking and problem solving. I distinctly remember awaking one night because I needed a drink of water. I had learned to leave a glass on my night stand, so I took a sip and put my head back down on the pillow. Instead of dozing back off to sleep, I was up, my brain was wired and ready to begin the day. Instead of tossing and turning and frustrating myself over the fact I was awake and really needed to be asleep, I got up, grabbed my sketchbook, turned the dimmer switch on low, and wrote down every thought that popped into my mind. I filled close to three pages full of thoughts. When I couldn't think of another word to put on the page, I closed the sketchbook, went back to bed, and sawed logs until morning.

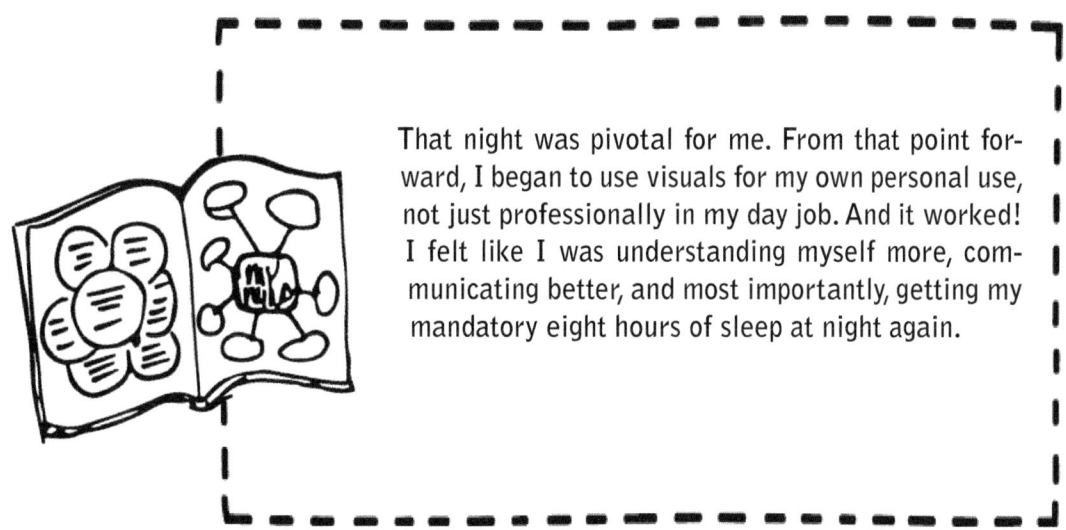

That night was pivotal for me. From that point forward, I began to use visuals for my own personal use, not just professionally in my day job. And it worked! I felt like I was understanding myself more, communicating better, and most importantly, getting my mandatory eight hours of sleep at night again.

Over the next few years, I developed as a person and as a visual problem solver. Any sort of challenge I faced was a new opportunity to create a visual tool. When I began to realize that a lot of other people had the same troubles sleeping as I did, I was inspired to try to solve their struggles with visual tools. To my friends that were struggling with insomnia, I suggested they mind-map their thoughts as I had started to years before. In the meantime, I started to sketch different visual tools that could be useful for people to clear their minds before bed.

Over the next few months, I sketched ideas for a multitude of visual tools that could be used, and eventually, I came to a point where I could package a set of simple visual tools into a mini booklet that others could use to capture their thoughts, relieve their stress, and get some sleep.

I can't say I get great sleep every night—I haven't found a visual tool that will stop my neighbor's dogs from barking or keep my son from having nightmares—but now I feel more in control of my brain instead of it controlling me and my sleep. I have gained that control through a combination of learning to be more self-aware, employing useful tools, and making good choices for myself.

There are times when I still wake up in the middle of the night with a list of to-dos or stay up later than I should scrolling through Instagram. But now, when that occurs, I realize I have not been taking the time to capture what is on my mind in a proactive way. So I move back to using my set of visual tools to capture my thoughts, prepare before bed time, and switch my brain back to sleep mode as quickly as possible.

So I commend you on taking the first step in getting back the sleep you deserve! I realize your life is crazy busy and you are trying to maximize the hours you are awake – I created this book with that in mind. This book is separated into four sections – one for each of the sleep archetypes – so once you identify which sleep archetype to focus on first, jump directly to that section. Each section is designed to exhaust your thoughts for that particular archetype so that by day seven your mind feels clearer, less overwhelmed, more aware of what you need to thrive and most importantly you are able to fall asleep and stay asleep. By completing each template, you are capturing your important thoughts, making space to understand them and building on those thoughts for the 7 days. By day 7, you should be able to create a plan to act on when you wake up the next day but also begin to build these template activities into your daily life. Before you know it, you will be sound asleep instead of wide awake.

The Sleepless Archetypes

As we relax and prepare to drift off to sleep, our brain waves are moving from alpha to theta state—it's a state where creativity flourishes, our memory is at its peak performance, and we are relaxed. Normally, we then drop off to sleep in the delta state. Our brains are complex, though, and our thoughts can stop us from moving into that meditative state.

During different times in my life, as I struggled to find sleep, I noticed those thoughts seemed to surface into four distinct forms:

WORRIER

ME MOMENTS

IDEA MAKER

TO-DOER

The Idea Maker

Throughout the day, an idea maker may struggle to find their creative zone, and then, as their head hits the pillow, bam! A wave of possibilities come rushing into their brains. They could build a business in one night! And maybe they should! Losing the beginnings of an awesome idea are so frustrating. Sometimes you want to roll over and just go to sleep, but everything seems so clear right then! Other times, they have so many ideas their brains are in overload.

You might often find yourself thinking..

"Oh, wow, this is such a great idea! I am such a foodie and I love making family traditions. I should merge the two and start a business to help other families create family food traditions..."

"Would I have a store front or offer services online? Maybe I could get my family to bake items to sell if it was a store... and Aunt Ginny is a nutritionist so maybe she could offer services out of the shop too..."

To-Doers

A to-doer is a person who puts their head on the pillow and instead of falling off to sleep blissfully, the long, long, infinite list of ALL the things that need to happen run through their brain. If they manage to actually get to sleep, they wake up in the middle of sleep (for whatever reason—heard a noise like their husband snoring, or had to pee cause they drank wayyyy too much water before bed, even though its good for you—yeah thats me, might not be everyone!) and that list runs through their minds. It gets them so fired up they can't fall back asleep, but they aren't coherent enough to actually complete all the to-dos.

To-doers feel like their to-do list is never ending. Seems to-doers are constantly crossing things off their lists, but always coming up with more to accomplish. They are passionate and busy, but they need some good shut-eye too!

As they begin to relax and settle in for a good nights rest, their brain waves move from alpha to theta and the to-do flood gates burst open…

> I need to make a doctors appointment tomorrow, oh, and I might as well call the dentist too, and come to think of it, I should make a vet appointment for the dog….oh, I need to order more dog food, and while I am on Amazon, I should order more cacao nibs, which reminds me, I wanted to make smoothies for lunch tomorrow so I probably need to buy more frozen mangoes. My daughter loves mangoes…oh, she needed me to drop her off at work tomorrow so I better set my alarm a little earlier…

me moments

Often, others spend their time worrying and caring for everyone else. With your focus elsewhere, you forget about the most important thing—YOU! Me-moment types might feel a bit angry or resentful for never putting themselves first, or they may see it as the first opportunity to be alone. Either way, if you are awake, make it worth your while and focus on you. Where does your brain need to be so you can be ready to take on the day tomorrow? Complete the other sections first, exhaust all your thoughts about others, then move to you.

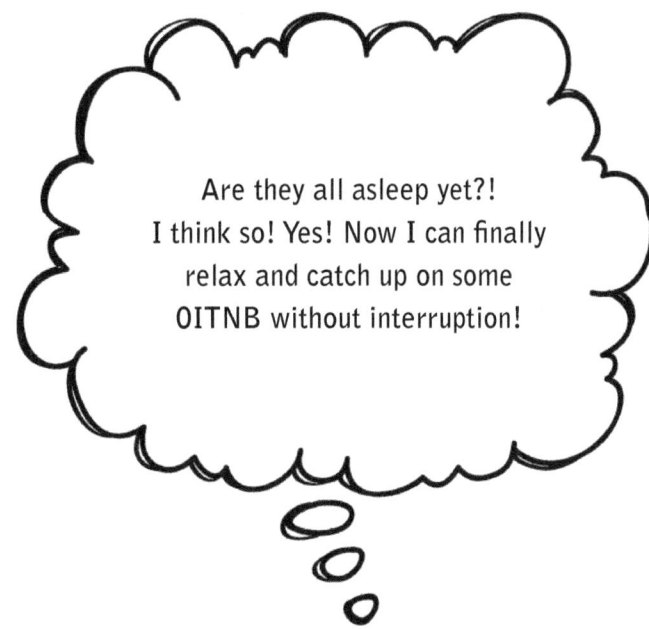

The Worriers

Worriers are in a state of anxiety, fear or doubt, fretting over the uncertainty of what is to come and what has already occurred. They could of, should of, would of the past...if only they had a time machine.

Then they focus on the endless possibilities of "what if" scenarios for the future. It is exhausting, but not exhausting enough to put them to sleep. Instead of being in the present moment of sleep, their anxiety kicks in about everything they can't control.

Sleep evades them as they think about everything but the present moment...

> I have so much work to finish up tomorrow. How am I ever going to finish it all? What if I put all that time into the work and my client doesn't like it? I wonder if they will refuse to pay? If they don't pay, how will I be able to pay my bills this month? I might lose my house! Where would I go?! I can't go to my parents....oh, what will my mother say? I can't go through another argument with her about getting a real job. Last time she made a comment, I should have said....

WHICH SLEEP ARCHETYPE ARE YOU?

Take the quiz to find out!

* Determine which archetype you are exhibiting.

* Read each set of scenarios.

* Check the box for each archetype you can closely relate to.

WHEN I CAN'T FALL ASLEEP OR

* My memory starts to actually work and I recall all of the things I was supposed to finish that day, but didn't.
* I think about what the next day will bring, and the list of action items I need to complete.

☐ **I am a To-Doer**

- -

* I am thinking so clearly with many ideas bouncing around in my mind.
* I am so busy with day-to-day life, I use this time to generate creative ideas.

☐ **I am an Idea maker**

STAY ASLEEP, IT IS BECAUSE:

* I am replaying a conversation from earlier today over and over again in my mind.
* I am thinking about the future, and what kind of world my kids will grow up in.

☐ **I am a Worrier**

---

* This is the first opportunity I have to catch up on my favorite TV show or book.
* I feel like I haven't done anything for myself that day, so I use this time for me.

☐ **I am a me moment**

TO-DOER > PAGE 17

WORRIER > PAGE 33

IDEA MAKER > PAGE 49

ME MOMENT > PAGE 65

MY ARCHETYPE is:
_____

NOW THAT YOU KNOW YOUR ARCHETYPE,
GO TO THE INDICATED PAGE TO
START YOUR 7-DAY PROGRAM
AND GET SOME

Zzzzzzzz...

Day 1:
LET'S GET CONNECTED

List all the people you need to connect with, whether by email, phone, or face-to-face meeting, and then why you need to connect with them (maybe dr. appointment, girls' night, message to kids teacher, etc.).

* In the WHO column, write down the person/organization's name.
* In the WHY column, write down what you need to discuss.

let's get connected

To-Doer

WHO	WHY

Day 2:
MAINTAIN

There is so much in our everyday life that just needs maintained (cutting the grass, cleaning, changing the oil, repainting base boards, planting the garden, dentist appointment, etc.), and of course, it's 3am when you remember the dog needs to go to the vet for his check-up.

This is the place to write it down.
* Think about different areas of your home.
* List all the maintenance to-dos for each area.
* Assign how often the to-do needs to be repeated.

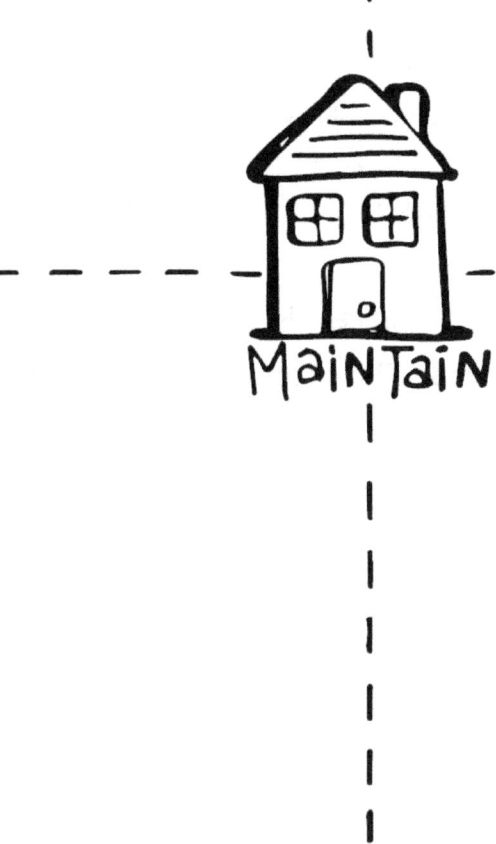

To-Doer

Day 3: BUY + SELL

I am always remembering the stuff I needed to order from Amazon (because I am obsessed with buying everyday stuff from there—introverts love to shop online!), which then reminds me I need to get rid of all the junk already in my house (clothes, toys, a blender I never use, things I can collect and drop off at Goodwill store).

* Write down all the items you need to purchase in the BUY tag.
* Write down all the items you need to sell (or donate) in the SELL tag.

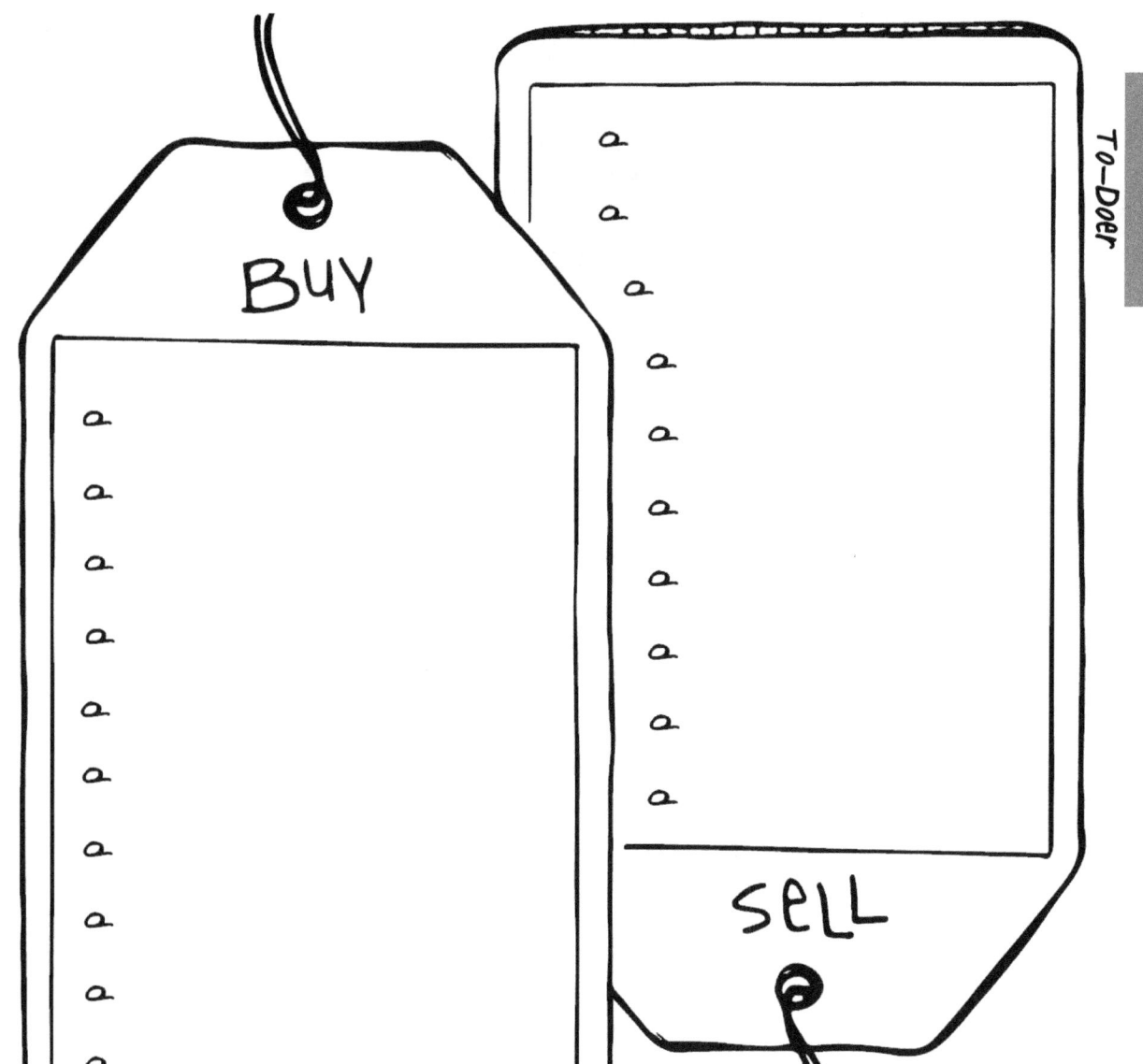

Day 4:
ME

You are so busy doing things for everyone else, you sometimes forget about the most important person—yourself.

* This is a space to write down all the to-dos that YOU need.

Day 5:
EMPTY YOUR MIND

After you get the immediate to-dos (within the next week or month) listed, then there are those far off to-dos that you thought you would never get to, but they are filling up space in your head.

This is a free-for-all to-do brain dump. Write down any crazy to-do that has crossed your mind that you may, at some point in your life, want to do—just get it out so you can have a clean mind to work from. Maybe it's organizing all your books alphabetically, comparing pet insurance plans to see if you are getting a good deal, or once-and-for-all getting the garage organized, researching costs for beach vacations, etc.

*   Write each to-do in a circle.

Day 6: MORNING PREP

Take a look at all the things that need done the next morning that you could do the night before or at least prep for so it isn't as much work in the morning. If you aren't getting enough sleep then you are probably groggy in the morning, and the brain isn't working at 100% yet so the less thinking you do, the better. Maybe it's packing your lunch, prepping breakfast, finding your kids' library books that are due the next day, etc.

* Write in all the actions you can do to make your morning run smoother.

MORNING PREP

To-Doer

→
→
→
→
→
→
→

→
→
→
→
→
→
→

Day 7: PLAN YOUR DAY

Now that you have listed all your to-dos (hopefully), let's plan when they can get done.

* Some won't be for tomorrow, but write in the ones that are.
* Plot them for a different part of the day based on what your schedule looks like.

Sometimes, I write in a slot for getting a shower! I know I will get one right after exercising so I plug it in along with eating lunch then look to see what to-dos can fit. I also normally write times. This can be repeated everyday.

* Just keep looking at the to-do lists, cross off what is done, and write in what needs to still be done. When there aren't any more to-dos on paper, I am sure your brain has come up with another long list.

PLAN YOUR DAY

MORNING

→
→
→
→

→
→
→
→

AFTERNOON

→
→
→
→

→
→
→
→

EVENING

→
→
→
→

→
→
→
→

To-Doer

Day 1:
BUBBLING UP

Past emotions can linger for quite some time and get in the way of sleep or your life in general. When those feelings are ignored, often times, they bubble up and turn into a toxic mixture of resentment, anger and guilt. Instead of letting those feelings fester inside, name them and move on.

* Write down a feeling you can't seem to shake on each line.
* Add any details in the space under the line.

What's Bubbling Up?

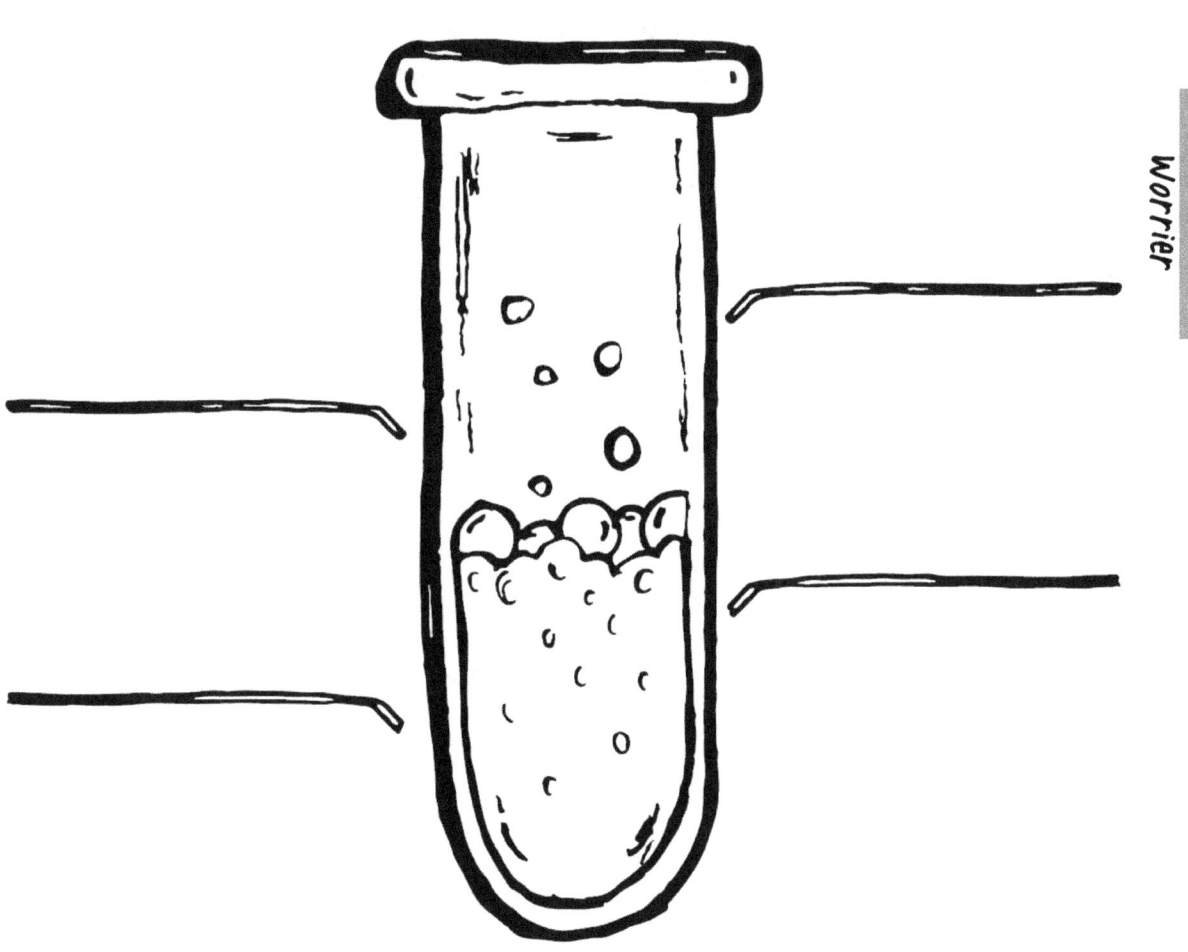

worrier

Day 2:
LET IT GO

Now, choose a past event/feeling that isn't serving you anymore.

* It is what it is, as they say. Take all your negative feelings around it and write them down.
* Now let it go. Let it glide right through your fingers and take a sigh of relief.
* It is gone and the past isn't holding you back anymore.

Day 3: PRO VS. CON

We make decisions every day—on how we will behave, who we will be, what we will do. Some decisions are bigger than others and need a little analysis. Use this to see both sides of the decision and then make it.

* Write down all the positive things about the decision in the top box.
* Write down all the negative things about the decision in the bottom box.

Worrier

 PRO vs CON

Day 4:
LET'S CHAT

Is there a particular conversation you have been playing in your mind over and over again? Worried you might sound too harsh or too soft? Or if you even should say it?

Make room for something better in your headspace.

* Write out what you need to say here. Who do you need to talk to? What is it about?
* Unload it all on the paper, then decide if it needs to be said out loud and refine it. Think of this as a first draft.

Day 5:
FLIP IT

Sometimes you need to shift your attitude a bit.

* List some negative thoughts you have right now. What are you telling yourself you CAN'T do?
* Now, flip your CAN'T to a CAN. Write a positive thought to counter each of the negative ones.

Day 6:
IN CONTROL

When life seems to be out of our control, we can end up in a bad place. We may say and do things that really aren't like us. Often, we do have control over our worries and we are ALWAYS in control of our behaviors. We choose how we react to situations.

* List some worries you can control in the left hand column.
* Then, in the right hand column, list which actions you can take to lessen the worry.

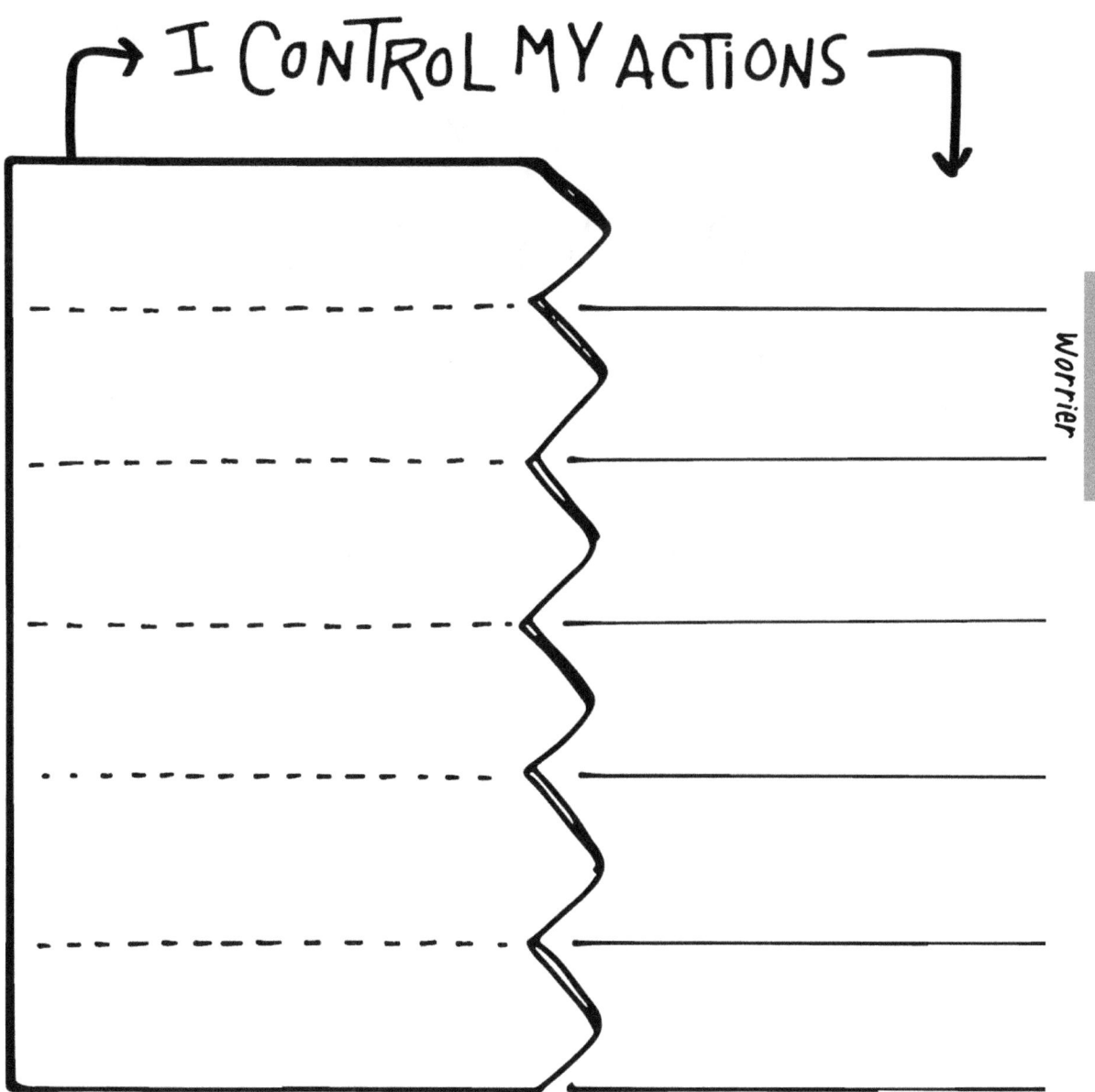

Day 7:
POSITIVE VIBES

There are some situations we really do not have control over. Sometimes all you can do is send a positive thought. It isn't your battle to take on, but you can be a concerned supporter.

* List your worry and then identify a wish or thought that can be sent. It is more productive than worrying and you can control what you send out into the world.

Day 1:
WHATCHA THINKING?

Ideas run through our minds constantly and can keep us awake at night. It can be tiring and overwhelming trying to discern which is worth more development or not.

* Take some time to capture all your ideas—the good, the bad, and the way out there ones.
* Write each idea down in the thought bubble. These can be ideas that you want to make or create, plan or share with others, or just the beginnings of something that can be great.

Day 2: FREE ASSOCIATION

Need to generate more ideas?

* Begin with a single word, theme, or topic. Write it in the middle circle.
* Now, take some time to let your mind wander. Write down the first word or thought that comes to mind.
* As you write one thought down, another will pop up. Continue writing each word, even if it doesn't seem to connect, until all the boxes are filled.
* Ponder what you captured and ask yourself if you see any new connections? Are any new ideas forming based on the free associations?

idea maker

Day 3:
IDEA SEEDS

Some thoughts you generate may be so newly formed that they need more space to grow into something tangible. If that little seed of a new idea is so difficult to even put into words, try giving them a little space to grow.

* Stop the ideas from tumbling around in your mind and write them down in each box.
* More time might be needed to grow it stronger, so come back to this page when you are ready to choose an idea to focus on.
* But first, get some zzz's.

Day 4: FOCUS

When you have an idea seed growing, the details seem far off. Take some time to really FOCUS on that one idea.

* Write the idea in the magnifying glass. In each section, capture anything and everything that you know about that idea.
* Do the details seem a bit clearer?

Idea maker

Day 5: REALITY CHECK

Once you have a healthy amount of ideas generated, you will want to prioritize them. Some of those ideas will most likely get cut. The remaining ideas will be competing for your attention. It isn't realistic to try to build out all of the ideas at once, and it can be tricky to determine which to choose first. We can become too close to a certain idea, and often, we may need a reality check.

* Scan through all the ideas you have generated thus far and number any that seem ready to be developed further.
* Now, plot each number (which corresponds with the idea) in one of the quadrants on the matrix. The bottom left would be considered "low" on both axes. The top right would be considered "high" on both axes.
* Take into consideration both the time commitment and resources needed before plotting the number. Ask yourself: Will I need to spend a lot of time and energy developing this idea further?
* Now, consider the amount of resources (financial and other) that are required to develop the idea. Would you consider the amount low or high?

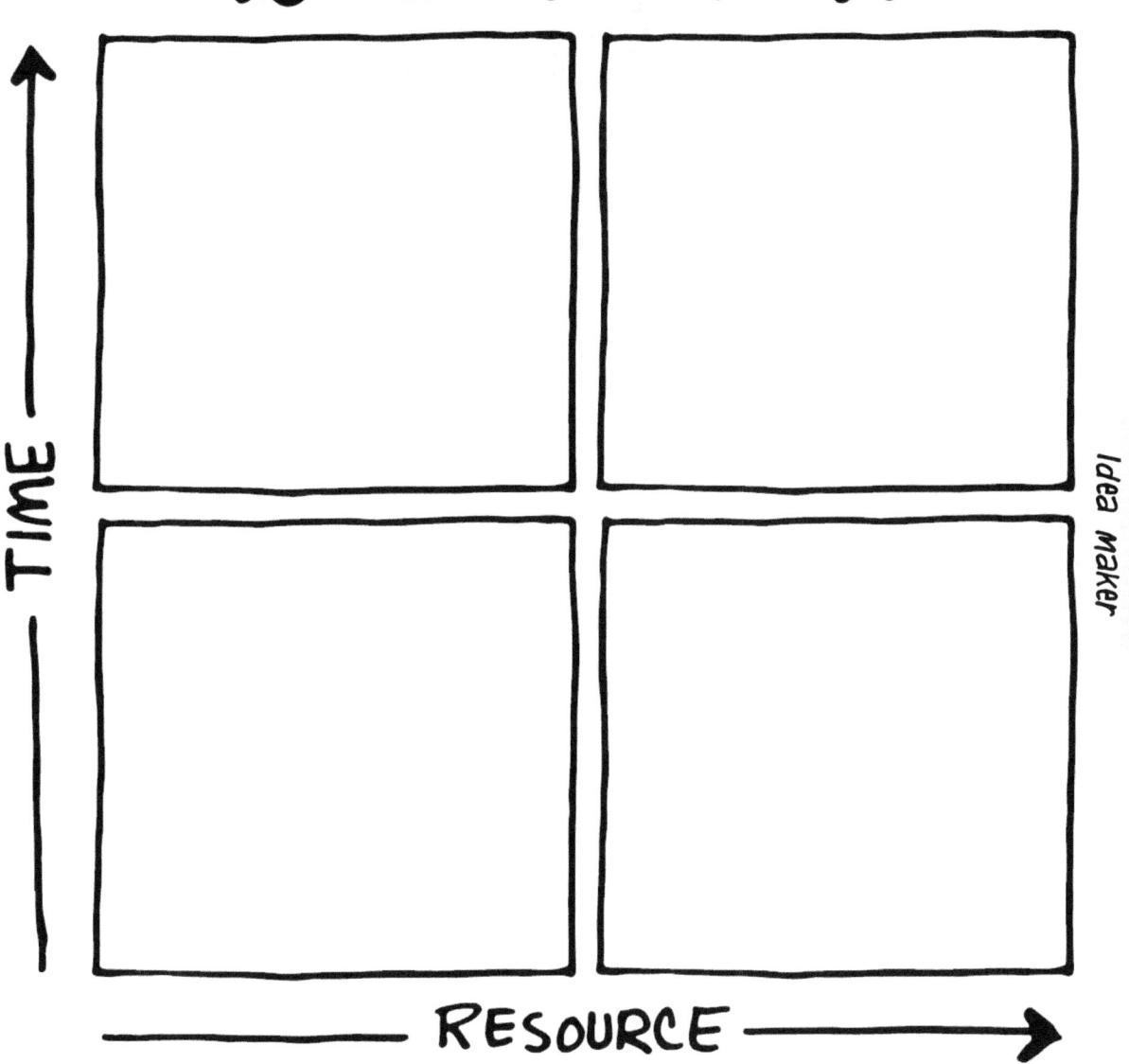

Day 6: ACTION

Deciding on an idea is an exciting feeling. Once you make that decision, you are ready to move into action! You can probably come up with a long list of to-dos and that can become overwhelming very quickly. Try taking it on in small bites with a little planning.

Choose one idea that is ready for development and can be realistically accomplished in the time frame you have and with the resources available. Fill in the IDEA box with the one you chose. Now, think about the immediate next steps you need to take to develop your idea.

* List the first three steps and try to add as many details as possible.
* Next, write a realistic date by when this task will be completed.
* Last, write in names of people who you will need to assist with the task.
* You now have a mini action plan in place. Once you finish those three steps, add in the next three.

ACTION

IDEA:

NEXT STEPS	BY WHEN	WHO

Idea maker

Day 7: IDEA MOJO

Even if you are comfortable with being creative, we all have blocks from time to time. Often, we get stuck in the day-to-day rut and we need to shake things up. Take some time to think about the situations where you are most creative and able to develop new ideas easily.

Fill in each section to determine what works for you.

* WHEN do you have light bulb moments? Is it a certain time of day, a season?
* WHERE do you feel most creative to form ideas? Are you indoors or outdoors? Are you in nature or a bustling city?
* WHO energizes you to generate ideas? Do you have a group of inspirational people you like to meet up with? Or do you need a quiet space away from others?
* WHAT type of activities spark ideas for you? Is it a brisk walk around the block, a yoga session, listening to music, or possibly just taking a shower?

WHO

WHAT

WHERE

WHEN

IDEA MOJO

Idea maker

Day 1: REFLECTION

There is no one to distract you now, so focus on you. When you look at yourself, who do you see?

* Write down some words that describe who you are. How do you feel about those words?
* How do you want to describe yourself?
* Are you being kind to yourself?

me moments

Day 2: MY VALUES

Our values are at the core of every decision, action, and thought we have. We feel most authentic when our lives are aligned with those values. Take some time to think about what matters most to you, both personally or professionally.

* Write a descriptor word in each box. How do you want to describe yourself?
* Add some extra notes underneath to describe further how you choose to live your life.

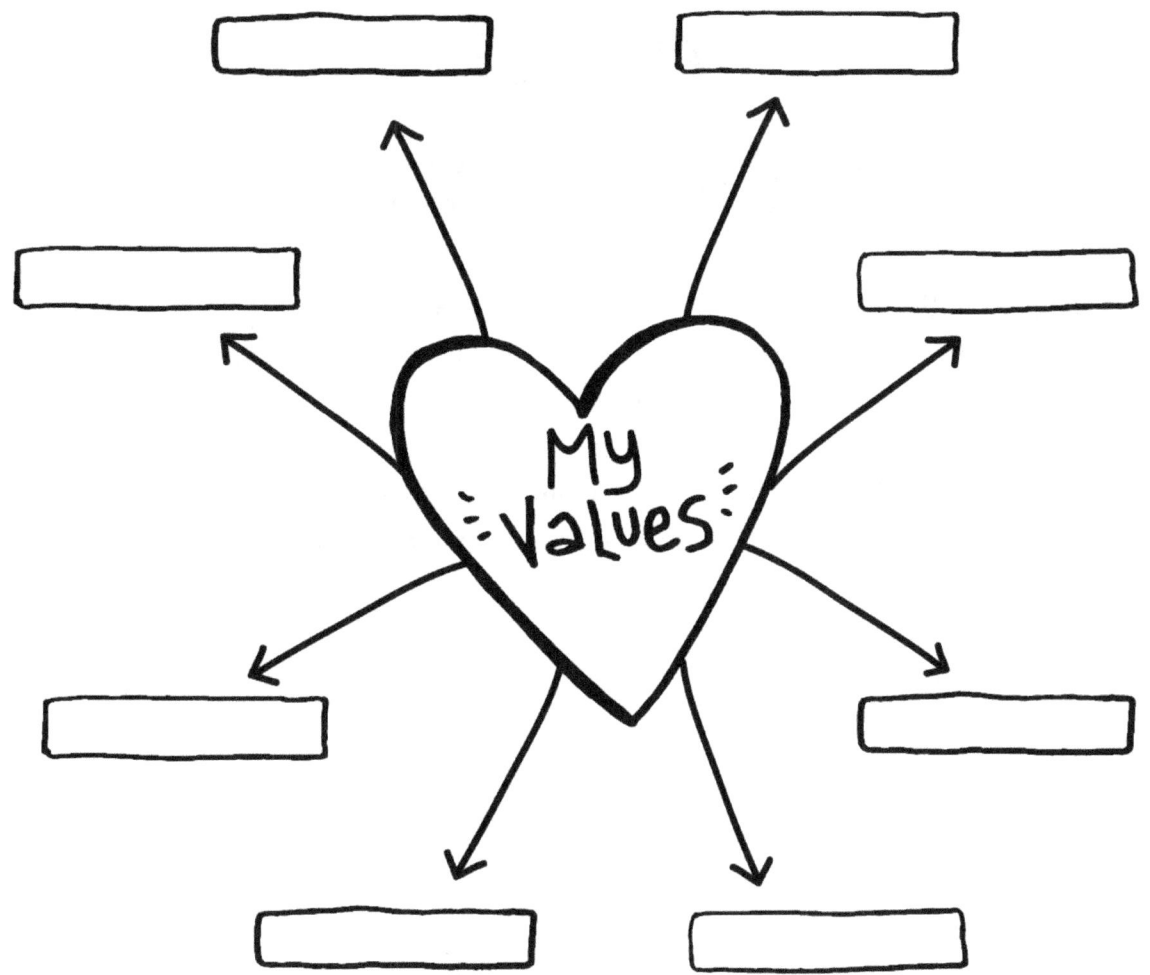

Day 3: WHOLE HEALTH

I just want to put this out there: *You are first and most important in your life.* **Putting yourself first is a necessity.** It is not being selfish. If you are not healthy and whole, you are not able to give to others, get things done, and truly live.

* Take some time to list what you need to be healthy and whole for your body (physical being), mind (mindset and perspective), and spirit (core values and beliefs).

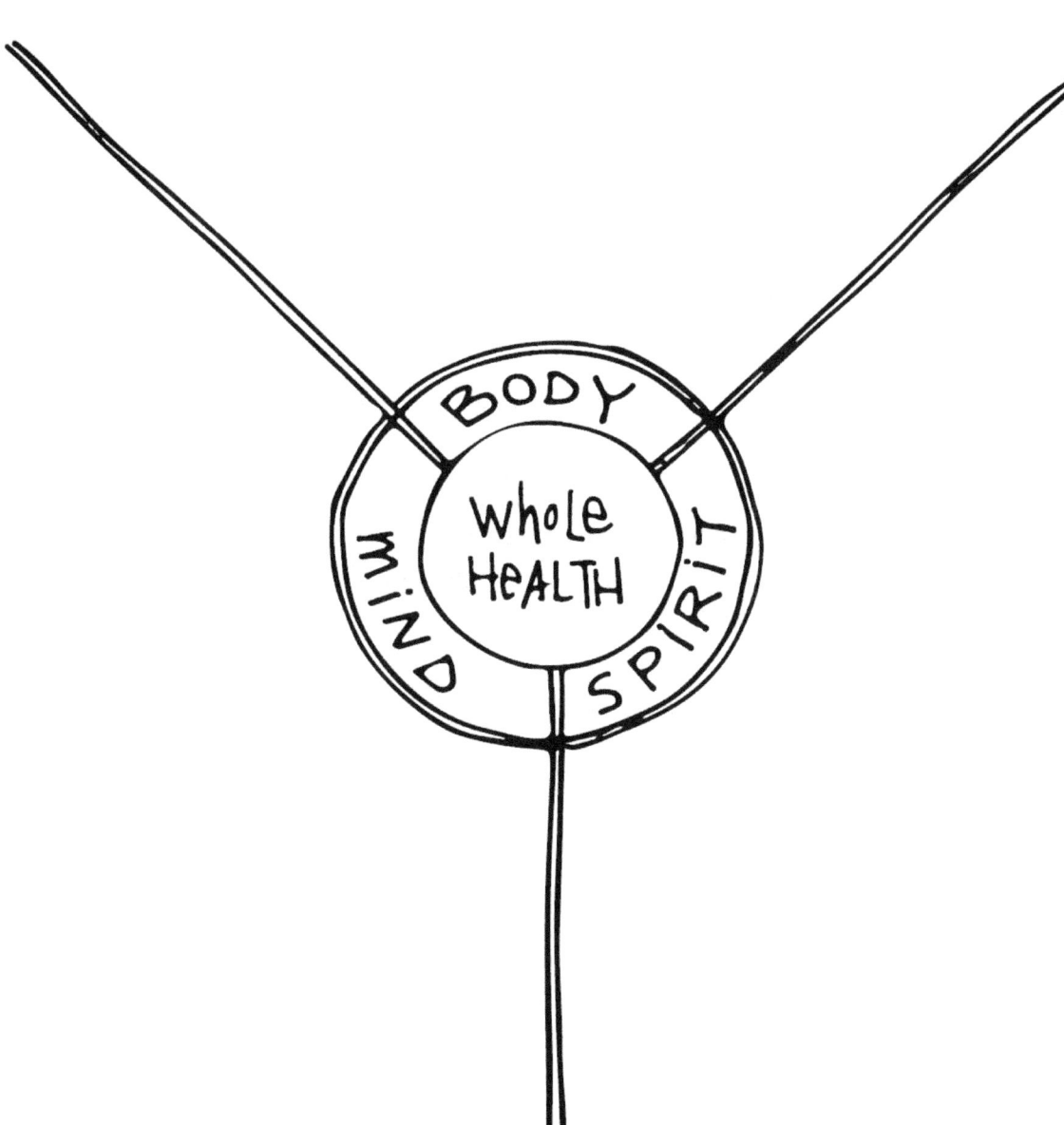

Day 4:
BE A MAGNET

What you think is what you attract. You are a magnet.

* Take time to write down something you want to attract in your life.
* List one thing in each title section. Underneath each section, brainstorm a list of ideas on how you can attract more of that particular thing in your life.

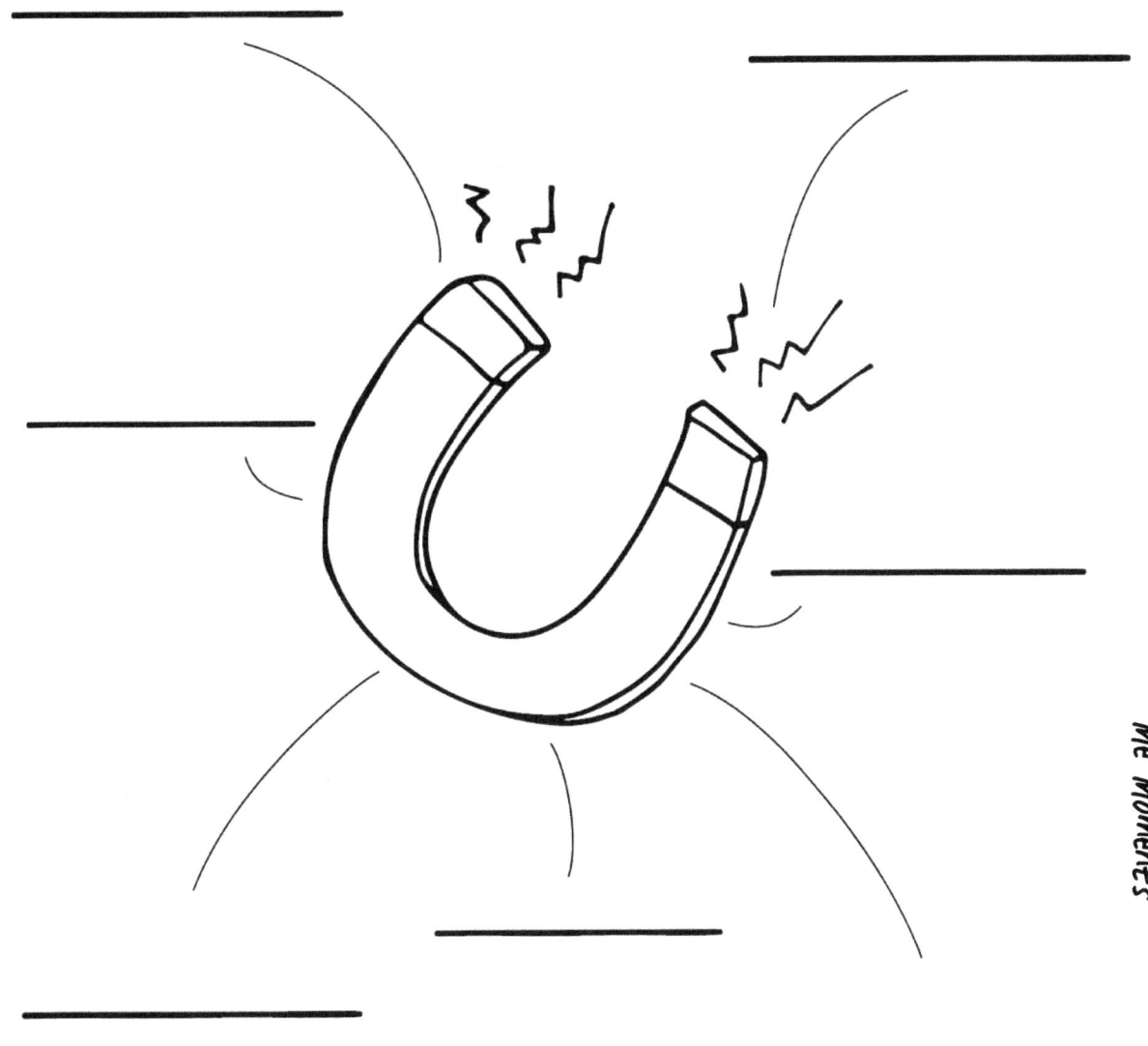

Day 5:
I AM GRATEFUL

There may be plenty that you want, but you also already have a lot in your life.

* Take some time to identify what you currently have in your life that you are grateful for.

i am GRateful

♡ _____

because _____

♡ _____

because _____

♡ _____

because _____

me moments

Day 6: ME DAY

I know, it sounds crazy, but you are allowed to take time for yourself—in fact, it is encouraged! You may be super busy and have others relying on you, but, I promise, it will be the best thing to happen for everyone. Imagine there are no limitations, you have an endless supply of money and energy within a 24-hour period.

* What would that day look like for you? Imagine there are no limitations, you have an endless supply of money and energy within a 24-hour period.
* Now choose one activity you listed and work it into your schedule for next week.

MORNING

AFTERNOON

EVENING

Me Moments

Day 7:
GOLD STARS

Some days, it feels like our wheels are just spinning in place and we haven't accomplished a thing. Give yourself some credit though—it's been a long week and you have probably learned and done so much.

* List some accomplishments from this past week.

MY G☆LD STARS

☆ _____

☆ _____

☆ _____

☆ _____

☆ _____

Now you have the tools to help calm your mind's night chatter. Anticipate needing different tools at different times. Depending on what is going on in my life at the moment, I move between the different archetypes, using the tools that are most relevant at that specific time.

Be aware that retraining your brain takes time. It could take only one week of using visual tools to help you find your sleep again, but you could also need more time. These tools are the starting point for you to begin forming a healthy habit of capturing your thoughts before your sleep is affected. Habits are formed and broken slowly. It normally takes 21 days to make an action stick.

I encourage you to continue using these templates as needed and adopt the ones that work for you into your regular routine. Keep this workbook, a journal, or even a few sheets of paper with a pen in reaching distance from your bed. As soon as you feel that night chatter starting up, even if your head is already cozy on your pillow and the lights are out, begin filling in the relevant templates and capture your thoughts so your mind can quiet quickly.

Eventually, you will learn to listen to your mind, recognize what your brain needs to remain silent, and become proactive with using the tools that work. As you make better choices, you will gain control of your mind, instead of your mind overtaking you and your sleep.

ABOUT EMILY

Emily Marko is a visual storyteller who helps passionate business owners just like you solve complex problems with pictures. Life and business can get messy! Emily's an expert at using visuals to help you capture ideas, build action plans, share stories, and move from chaos to calm. She's a mix of strategist, coach, and artist, and has been helping clients get clear and take action for over 15 years. Discover how you can organize your brain and solve problems by visiting emilymarko.com.

www.ingramcontent.com/pod-product-compliance
Lightning Source LLC
Chambersburg PA
CBHW060503240426
43661CB00007B/898